Buddy Bee Discovers Fossil Rim

Written by Miles F. Price
and Illustrated by Greg Armstrong

© 2015 Buddy's World and Friends. All rights reserved.
www.buddysworldandfriends.com

This book is a dedication to two beautiful daughters both named Hayley (Haley). Each with the same first and middle proper name, with only a slight different spelling to the first name.

At a young age, Hayley and I shared some wonderful times and lasting memories together at Fossil Rim Wildlife Center located in Glen Rose, Texas.

The second Haley came along a few years after. Both have filled my life full of love. Each one has captured my heart.

Amazing. Someone up above "indeed" has a beautiful sense of timing and grace.

Buddy Bee's greatest hope: Is that a light will always shine upon all of Dad's "lil' girls. Thus allowing the same light to shine upon the love all Dad's give to their daughters unconditionally. (This dedication also includes sons!)

"May this wonderful light always shine!"
-Miles F. Price-

One beautiful sun filled morning, Buddy Bee was joyfully buzzing and flying in the nice breeze above an open field.

Buddy looks down and spots a small bird dancing happily in the field below. "A new friend!" Buddy exclaims. Buddy quickly buzzes down and begins to dance with his new friend.

"This is fun!" both Buddy and his new friend shout with glee.

"My name is Buddy Bee! What is your name?" Buddy is so very excited.

"Hi ya partner! My name is "Lil" Tex but all my friends here at Fossil Rim call me L.T.!" I am an Attwater Prairie Chicken.

"Friends?" says Buddy very curiously. "Yes, great friends, Buddy! You are so silly, Buddy!" laughs L.T. "Buddy you have buzzed in joyfully and landed at Fossil Rim Wildlife Center!" L.T. explains.

"Fossil Rim helped save my life, Buddy. All of my friends that we will meet here are so thankful for Fossil Rim! Buddy, are you ready to go meet your new friends?" L.T. is so happy!

"Yay!" says Buddy, and both L.T. and Buddy Bee began to embark on an exciting endangered wildlife adventure.

"Endangered means to place "at risk," friends!" L.T. felt the need to explain the word endangered to all of Buddy's friends.

The Attwater Prairie Chicken is possibly the most endangered bird in North America. Indians developed a dance that mimics the actions made by the male birds.

"First we will meet Allie." says L.T.

"Allie?" Buddy is very curious. "Allie always meets and greets all my new friends. Allie is an Ostrich and she is very curious too, Buddy. She likes to stare a lot. She is very friendly but please keep your hands to yourself until Allie gets to know you." L.T. explains.

"Hello Buddy, nice to meet you! Welcome to Fossil Rim!" Allie chirps with joy.

"Bob and Bessie are right around the bend in the pasture cooling off, Buddy. I cannot wait for you to meet them!" Allie is so thankful.

"Hey Buddy! C'mon in the mud is fine!" says Bob and Bessie.

"Bob and Bessie are two of our Southern Black Rhinos, Buddy" L.T. explains. Buddy Bee is so HapBee! Hello Bob and Bessie, it is great to meet you. I am so thankful we are friends."

Bob and Bessie are part of Fossil Rim's program to help save five types of Rhinos. Black Rhinos are from Zimbabwe, a country in Africa.

"Bingo!" A voice is heard coming from the outer part of the forest. "Who is that?" asks Buddy.

"Well look who is watching us! Buddy, meet Bingo the Bongo Antelope," says L.T.

"We are surprised to see you, Bingo. Buddy, Bingo the Bongo can hide really well." Explains L.T. "Bingo, you are so colorful. It is nice to meet you!" Buddy is amazed at Bingo's colorful fur.

"Thank you, Buddy! It is my pleasure." And without another word Bingo the Bongo Antelope takes off running and disappears into the forest.

Bingo the Bongo Antelope lives in West Central Africa. Bingo is the largest and most colorful antelope in the world.

"A giraffe! One of my best friends is a giraffe named Stanley. He has a cousin here at Fossil Rim named Jen." Buddy hopes to find Stanley's cousin.

"Guess what, Buddy? This is Jen!" L.T. is so surprised that out of all the giraffes living at Fossil Rim, the first one Buddy Bee meets is Stanley's Cousin, Jen. "Hey Jen, are you Stanley's cousin?" Buddy cannot believe it!

"As a matter of fact, Buddy, I am. Please give Stanley a big hug and a butterfly kiss from me," Jen was so happy. "Yay! I will make sure to tell Stanley," Buddy was beaming with glee.

Buddy was so excited to find Stanley's cousin. The giraffe is the tallest living land animal.

"L.T. wait for me! Andy the Aoudad - a wild African Sheep can be heard hollering from a distance. The Aoudad is native to Morocco and parts of the Western Sahara desert.

Andy after climbing up and over a rocky hillside appears upon the flat top of the hill. Andy can climb rocks a few hours right after birth.

"Wow, what a great climber you are! My name is Buddy and I am glad you caught up to us so that we can become friends," Buddy is amazed.

"Me too, Buddy! I love your red high tops!" Andy is so surprised that he discovers Buddy has on red high tops too!

L.T. and Buddy take a walk back to the campsite for lunch and discover Mannie, a Red wolf waiting for them by the campsite.

Suzy Camper who is a local resident also was at the campsite to welcome Buddy Bee and L.T.!

"What a pleasant surprise! Hey Mannie! Please say hello to our new friend Buddy Bee," L.T. is feeling so good about how his day is going with his new favorite friend.

"Whaooooo! Hey Buddy Bee! I could not wait to meet you! I heard from my friends here in the park that we have a new friend," howls Mannie.

Mannie - an expert tracker and hunter - followed Buddy and L.T. to the campsite.

Red wolves are known for the red color of their fur. They are social animals, living in small packs consisting of a pair, who will stay together for life.

The red wolf's diet consists mostly of white-tailed deer, raccoons, rabbits and rodents. Since most prey items are small mammals, red wolves do not have to rely solely on pack hunting, as do the gray and Mexican wolves. This species is generally shy and usually stays away from humans and human activities.

Fossil Rim has been a breeding facility for the Red Wolf since 1989 and has produced more than 30 pups. These wolves are housed in the Intensive Management Area and can be viewed on the Behind the Scenes Tours.

"I see a buffalo!" shouts Buddy.

"His name is Roman," explains L.T.

"Roman is so big and awesome. Hi Roman!" Buddy is amazed at Roman's size and strength.

"Home, home on the range!" Roman sings happily while chewing on some hay.

"Where the deer and antelope play!" Both L.T. and Buddy join in. All three start to smile and begin to laugh out loud!

"Buddy, I saw you buzzing joyfully around earlier and wanted to say "thank you" for coming down to Fossil Rim to see us," snorts Roman.

"Bison" or "Buffalo?"
"Buffalo" is the term used by most people to describe the American Bison. Buffalo are unpredictable and can be very dangerous. While appearing slow and docile, they are agile and can run as fast as a horse.

"Is your friend a horse with stripes?" Buddy notices another friend of L.T.'s from a distance.

"Buddy, you must be talking about Zoe the Zebra. Let us go down and see Zoe!" L.T. chuckles and smiles at Buddy.

Within an hour of birth, a baby Zebra can run with the rest of the herd and can recognize its mother with sight and smell. Each Zebra has a unique stripe pattern.

"Buddy, really now, a horse? I am a Zebra, silly bee. It was a really good question Buddy!" Zoe smiles.

"Zoe, make certain you tell all of our friends there is a party tonight at our campsite!" L.T. is happy yet is sad that this will be Buddy's last night at Fossil Rim.

"What a wonderful day today my friends! I want to give all of you my heartfelt thanks for your friendship and kindness."

"L.T., it was so much fun and I learned so very much about Fossil Rim," Buddy is so very thankful for his new friends.

Already Buddy is looking forward to his next visit to see the friends he has made and most especially: an opportunity to make new friends. Happy times ahead!

"Buddy, we are friends for life. Please bring some of your special friends in Buddy's World next time with you. We cannot wait to meet them!" answers L.T.

"We love you, Buddy!" all of Buddy's new friends say together. "I love you all and will see you soon!" Buddy has had a fun and exciting day at Fossil Rim.

Buddy and his friends end the night roasting marshmallows, laughing and sharing wonderful stories around the campfire.

"Sssshhhh, Bob and Bessie are fast asleep."

"Good night friends. Sweet dreams."

What a great adventure! A wonderful new beginning!

"Thank you, Fossil Rim!"

- Buddy Bee -

── The End ──

Fossil Rim is the first facility of its kind to have been accredited by the American Zoo and Aquarium Association.

Fossil Rim Wildlife Center participates in a worldwide network of wildlife conservation organizations working to restore the delicate balance between people, animals and the environment. Fossil Rim Wildlife Center represents over 1,000 animals, 50 species of native and non-native animals living peacefully at the ~1,700-acre center.

Fossil Rim's Vision:
We focus on the good stewardship of wildlife for the well-being of our planet, our children and the generations to come, supported through the participation of an informed and concerned public.

www.fossilrim.org

Buddy Bee's Vision:
To have the opportunity to become part of the life of the child through our characters. Assisting in the development of creativity and learning through imagination. Creativity and continued learning is so very critical for both the young and the old alike!

www.buddysworldandfriends.com

In loving memory of "Sherlock" the Deer.

Sherlock gave Hayley and Daddy a nightly visit at the Fossil Rim campsite. A very loving and special animal.

We miss you Sherlock!

This book has such special meaning:

Thank you Greg for the wonderful drawings. Your friendship and creativity is truly inspirational.

Thank you Haley for being such a wonderful daughter. I am very proud of the person you have become.

Thanks to my folks who recently celebrated their 61st anniversary.

Thanks to Big Sis, David and Tarah!

Thanks Mama!

Thank you HB! Thank you Big!

Thank you Lyndell Joy, my love, so blessed.

"It is "indeed" all about the child."

- Buddy Bee -

www.ingramcontent.com/pod-product-compliance
Lightning Source LLC
LaVergne TN
LVHW010020070426
835507LV00001B/13